GREAT

AMERICAN PRESIDENTS

HARRY S.
TRUMAN

GREAT AMERICAN PRESIDENTS

JOHN ADAMS

JOHN QUINCY ADAMS

JIMMY CARTER

THOMAS JEFFERSON

JOHN F. KENNEDY

ABRAHAM LINCOLN

RONALD REAGAN

FRANKLIN DELANO ROOSEVELT

THEODORE ROOSEVELT

HARRY S. TRUMAN

GEORGE WASHINGTON

WOODROW WILSON

—————— GREAT——————
AMERICAN PRESIDENTS

HARRY S.
TRUMAN

MICHAEL FOLEY

FOREWORD BY
WALTER CRONKITE

CHELSEA HOUSE
PUBLISHERS
A Haights Cross Communications Company

Philadelphia

CHELSEA HOUSE PUBLISHERS

VP, NEW PRODUCT DEVELOPMENT Sally Cheney
DIRECTOR OF PRODUCTION Kim Shinners
CREATIVE MANAGER Takeshi Takahashi
MANUFACTURING MANAGER Diann Grasse

STAFF FOR HARRY S. TRUMAN

ASSOCIATE EDITOR Kate Sullivan
PRODUCTION EDITOR Megan Emery
ASSISTANT PHOTO EDITOR Noelle Nardone
SERIES DESIGNER Keith Trego
COVER DESIGNER Keith Trego
LAYOUT 21st Century Publishing and Communications, Inc.

A Haights Cross Communications Company

www.chelseahouse.com

First Printing

1 3 5 7 9 8 6 4 2

Library of Congress Cataloging-in-Publication Data

Foley, Michael, 1948-
  Harry Truman / by Michael Foley.
    p. cm. -- (Great American presidents)
Summary: A biography of Harry Truman, thirty-third President of the
United States, who dropped atomic bombs on Japan to end World War II
and dealt with other problems left by the death of Franklin Roosevelt.
Includes bibliographical references and index.
  ISBN 0-7910-7596-6
 1. Truman, Harry S., 1884-1972--Juvenile literature. 2. Presidents--United
States--Biography--Juvenile literature. [1. Truman, Harry S., 1884-1972. 2.
Presidents.] I. Title. II. Series.
  E814.F65 2003
  973.918'092--dc22

                                                  2003014419

TABLE OF CONTENTS

FOREWORD:
   WALTER CRONKITE   6

1   HARDWORKING AMERICAN   10

2   ROOSEVELT'S INHERITANCE   20

3   THE BOMB   28

4   AFTER THE WAR   38

5   TRUMAN'S TRIUMPH   48

6   FAIR DEAL   62

7   THE RISING RED SCARE   72

TIMELINE: THE PRESIDENTS OF THE UNITED STATES   90

PRESIDENTIAL FACT FILE   92

PRESIDENT TRUMAN IN PROFILE   95

CHRONOLOGY   97

BIBLIOGRAPHY   99

FURTHER READING   100

INDEX   101

FOREWORD

WALTER CRONKITE

A candle can defy the darkness. It need not have the power of a great searchlight to be a welcome break from the gloom of night. So it goes in the assessment of leadership. He who lights the candle may not have the skill or imagination to turn the light that flickers for a moment into a perpetual glow, but history will assign credit to the degree it is due.

Some of our great American presidents may have had a single moment that bridged the chasm between the ordinary and the exceptional. Others may have assured their lofty place in our history through the sum total of their accomplishments.

When asked who were our greatest presidents, we cannot fail to open our list with the Founding Fathers who put together this nation and nursed it through the difficult years of its infancy. George Washington, John Adams, Thomas Jefferson, and James Madison took the high principles of the revolution against British tyranny and turned the concept of democracy into a nation that became the beacon of hope to oppressed peoples around the globe.

Almost invariably we add to that list our wartime presidents—Abraham Lincoln, perhaps Woodrow Wilson, and certainly Franklin Delano Roosevelt.

Nonetheless there is a thread of irony that runs through the inclusion of the names of those wartime presidents: In many aspects their leadership was enhanced by the fact that, without objection from the people, they assumed extraordinary powers to pursue victory over the nation's enemies (or, in the case of Lincoln, the Southern states).

The complexities of the democratic procedures by which the United States Constitution deliberately tried to withhold unchecked power from the presidency encumbered the presidents who needed their hands freed of the entangling bureaucracy that is the federal government.

Much of our history is written far after the events themselves took place. History may be amended by a much later generation seeking a precedent to justify an action considered necessary at the latter time. The history, in a sense, becomes what later generations interpret it to be.

President Jefferson in 1803 negotiated the purchase of vast lands in the south and west of North America from the French. The deal became knows as the Louisiana Purchase. A century and a half later, to justify seizing the nation's steel mills that were being shut down by a labor strike, President Truman cited the Louisiana Purchase as a case when the president in a major matter ignored Congress and acted almost solely on his own authority.

The case went to the Supreme Court, which overturned Truman six to three. The chief justice, Fred Vinson, was one of the three justices who supported the president. Many historians, however, agreed with the court's majority, pointing out that Jefferson scarcely acted alone: Members of Congress were in the forefront of the agitation to consummate the Louisiana Purchase and Congress voted to fund it.

With more than two centuries of history and precedent now behind us, the Constitution is still found to be flexible when honest and sincere individuals support their own causes with quite different readings of it. These are the questions that end up for interpretation by the Supreme Court.

As late as the early years of the twenty-first century, perhaps the most fateful decision any president ever can make—to commit the nation to war—was again debated and precedent ignored. The Constitution says that only the Congress has the authority to declare war. Yet the Congress, with the objection of few members, ignored this Constitutional provision and voted to give President George W. Bush the right to take the United States to war whenever and under whatever conditions he decided.

Thus a president's place in history may well be determined by how much power he seizes or is granted in re-interpreting and circumventing the remarkable document that is the Constitution. Although the Founding Fathers thought they had spelled out the president's authority in their clear division of powers between the branches of the executive, the legislative and the judiciary, their wisdom has been challenged frequently by ensuing generations. The need and the demand for change is dictated by the march of events, the vast alterations in society, the global condition beyond our influence, and the progress of technology far beyond the imaginations of any of the generations which preceded them.

The extent to which the powers of the presidency will be enhanced and utilized by the chief executives to come in large degree will depend, as they have throughout our history, on the character of the presidents themselves. The limitations on those powers, in turn, will depend on the strength and will of those other two legs of the three-legged stool of American government—the legislative and the judiciary.

And as long as this nation remains a democracy, the final say will rest with an educated electorate in perpetual exercise of its constitutional rights to free speech and a free and alert press.

HARDWORKING
AMERICAN

HARRY S. TRUMAN, the 33rd president of the United States, spent his early life in the western part of Missouri with neither substantial trauma nor brilliance. His parents, John Anderson Truman and Martha Ellen Young, generally lived a moderate life. John Truman held various jobs, from farmer to night watchman, depending on his financial situation and geographic location. He never achieved great financial success. Truman's mother was supportive and strong-minded, and the family remained solid throughout its various relocations and endeavors.

Harry Truman was born on May 8, 1884, when the family was in the city of Lamar in Barton County, Missouri. They moved

The future president of the United States, Harry S. Truman had a rather nondescript childhood. He was born and raised in Missouri and had many interests as a child. His bad eyesight kept him from participating in sports, but he was a voracious reader.

twice in 1885 and then again in 1887 to stay at the Young family's large farm at Grandview. Here, John Truman assisted his father-in-law with managing the farm until the family moved to Independence, Missouri, where they would settle for a 12-year period. Throughout these formative years, Truman's parents provided him and his two younger siblings, John and Mary, with relatively proper schooling, music lessons, and other basic opportunities.

Truman pursued studies and music with great diligence.

His poor eyesight precluded him from boyhood sports, but his great interest in the piano and his extensive reading more than compensated. Still, his dedication—rather than actual achievements—is significant. Despite his surprising amounts of reading, he was not a prodigious scholar, nor was his skill with the piano worthy of any concert hall. The practical Truman seemed to recognize the limits of his abilities and made no substantial effort to pursue fantastical dreams of greatness.

Young Truman, however, was in no way a limited person; his experience with studies and music proved that he was a hardworking, industrious individual. He worked for his own sake, reading and playing piano regardless of external recognition. Steadfast industry and hard work: Even in his early years Truman seemed to fit the stereotype of America and its citizens.

After his father had a difficult financial year, the family moved to Kansas City. Truman could not go to college because of the new financial stress, and his eyesight barred him from his dream of military school at Annapolis or West Point. He remained in Kansas City, taking jobs from bank clerk to timekeeper for construction workers until the family moved back to the Grandview farm in 1906. Truman remained there until 1917, spending his twenties and early thirties as a farmer with little time for other significant pursuits—no college, military school, nor major political strides outside of joining the Masons, a secret society that networked its power to achieve the common goals and advancement of its members. Truman was in no way a major player of this group; he had neither the money for great influence nor the time away from the farm to fill a more "useful" role.

In staying at Grandview, Truman may have sacrificed a college experience and other possible pursuits of his youthful twenties, but he proved himself to be a man true to his family, willing to put in the long hours of a respectable farmer.

Truman did begin courting of his future wife and first lady, Elizabeth "Bess" Virginia Wallace. She was only a year younger than Truman, and they had been childhood classmates. Truman had always noticed her: She was pretty, athletic, and from a well-moneyed family. She could have her choice of many men, but Truman's character as an industrious Grandview family farmer would eventually win her over. The couple got engaged in 1917, and after his return

"I have found the best way to give advice to your children is to find out what they want and then advise them to do it."

— Harry S. Truman

from World War I, they married at ages 33 and 32. They had one child, Mary Margaret (born February 17, 1924), and were faithfully married until his death.

Although Truman had joined the National Guard in Kansas City, he did not see any substantial military action until World War I. For the short period before the war, he had attempted various small business endeavors, all of which failed in one way or another. The war would give him the chance to feel like a patriot and leave behind these failures.

Harry and Bess Truman were married on June 28, 1919, after Harry returned from World War I. They had one daughter, Mary Margaret, who was born on February 17, 1924.

He was elected first lieutenant of the 129th Field Artillery, trained with his men in Oklahoma, and was sent to France on March 30, 1918. He quickly became a captain and took command of Battery D. Although they were never at serious risk, the men of Battery D appreciated Truman's leadership, and he established great friendships based on this respect.

Truman returned to the United States in April 1919, pleased with his activity and accomplishments in fighting for his country. After marrying Bess in June, Truman set out with one of his war comrades to start a haberdashery business. This enterprise, which involved the sale of men's furnishings and other small items, eventually failed, as had all of Truman's past business attempts. The 1922 failure proved much worse, however, and Truman and his partner acquired a tremendous amount of debt. His partner filed for bankruptcy, but the stubborn, hardworking Truman worked years to eventually pay off his creditors.

POLITICAL BEGINNINGS

Another opportunity resulting from Truman's war experience presented itself in 1922, when Jim Pendergast, a man who served with Truman in World War I, approached him about the possibility of Truman becoming the county court judge of eastern Jackson County in Missouri. Running for this office could be successful with the endorsement of the Pendergasts, a family that had a great deal of political strength and influence at the time. Often referred to as the "Pendergast machine," their political networking would certainly make Truman a serious candidate. Truman accepted and won the tight race for the Democratic nomination that spring. He then went on to win the election in November.

Although he was not reelected in 1924, Truman enjoyed his first experience of public office. When approached by the Pendergasts in 1926 about running for presiding judge of the county court, he again accepted and won the election. In this position of considerable local power, Truman strove to perform great service for the county and do so honorably within the law. The people of Missouri increasingly recognized him as a hardworking, honest man.

Truman took to his role as a public official and wanted to advance to the U.S. Senate in 1934. However, this would be no easy task: state senator and governor are the most respected state government positions. The people of Missouri would certainly elect a Democrat over a Republican; the trouble would be winning the primary election to become the official candidate for the Democrats. He would need the backing of the Pendergasts, and they would need him: The Pendergast machine was known for its corruption, and only a man of Truman's character could counteract their reputation. Though they may have preferred other candidates and attempted to recruit them, Truman served as the ultimate compromise candidate.

Even with the eventual support of the Pendergasts, however, the campaign would be quite difficult. With his trademark dedication, Truman set out on an intense tour of the state, giving about ten speeches a day. Again his intensity paid off—he won the primary election for the Democrats, and in November of 1934, Harry S. Truman was elected to represent Missouri as a senator in the United States Congress.

Secure in the senate for six years, Truman pleased the presidential administration with his support of the

Harry Truman was elected to the United States Senate in November 1934. He had valuable support from the Pendergasts, a powerful Democratic family from Missouri. Truman did little during his first term in the Senate except support Roosevelt's New Deal, but he was able to win reelection in 1940, this time without the support of the Pendergasts.

New Deal. However, because he lacked any real power, he accomplished little else—he moved along for six years as a content, mediocre senator. In 1940, when Truman was up for reelection, he received minimal support from the now-broken Pendergast machine and the presidential administration. Again, Truman had to campaign strenuously, but he was ultimately able to capture the senatorial seat for another six years.

Now rooted more deeply in the Senate, Truman could take on powerful responsibilities. He became chairman of the Committee to Investigate the National Defense Program, which was in charge of evaluating government spending for production relating to World War II. Truman exposed and cleaned many of the inefficient war contracts. The country appreciated his close investigations, and although he was not the most extraordinary politician, more people began to respect him as an honest worker who had the country's best interest at heart.

> *"I always remember an epitaph which is in this cemetery at Tombstone, Arizona. It says: 'Here lies Jack Williams. He done his damnedest.' I think that is the greatest epitaph a man can have— When he gives everything that is in him to do the job he has before him. This is all you can ask of him and that is what I have tried to do."*
>
> — Harry S. Truman

When President Roosevelt ran for reelection in 1944, he had trouble finding a vice president. For complicated political reasons, his current vice president, Henry Wallace, was considered unable to carry enough votes, and the other main choices were strong-willed men who had irritated too many people. Truman would again suffice. No one seemed to disapprove strongly of him, so he would once more be a compromise candidate at the right place and time with the right reputation. He was not too bold, too sneaky, or too tied to one group over another. He was popular enough to be known but not popular enough to have people dislike him. Truman was not even too ambitious. Many were wary of Roosevelt's health and warier of how the other candidates considered themselves possible presidents if he died in office. Truman was hesitant in accepting the possible nomination for the vice presidency. He thought that the office was too vague and that the prospect of becoming president was too overwhelming.

President Roosevelt, when telephoned and informed of Truman's reluctance, delivered his now-famous response: "Tell [Truman] that if he wants to break up the Democratic party in the middle of the war, that is his responsibility." Truman accepted the proposal soon after this message was relayed to him, and the party agreed to an official nomination. Roosevelt and the Democrats prevailed in November, and on March 15, 1945, Truman was sworn in as vice president.

Without any spectacular skills or achievements, Harry S. Truman found himself at the president's side during America's greatest war. He did not win office through any brilliant proposals, powerful connections, or sly tactics. He certainly lacked the unstoppable charisma of politicians like President Roosevelt. He was simply Truman: the hardworking, dedicated, decent American.

2

ROOSEVELT'S INHERITANCE

PRESIDENT ROOSEVELT HAD long suffered from ill health. Afflicted with polio at the age of 39, he often retreated to his vacation home in Warm Springs, Georgia, to rest and release the tensions of his public responsibilities. It was while taking respite in his Warm Springs home in April 1945 that Roosevelt finally succumbed to the stress of over a decade as the nation's highest executive. On April 12, 1945, the 63-year-old president passed away.

In his more than 12 years of service as president of the United States, Franklin Roosevelt led the nation through the seemingly hopeless Great Depression and most of the war that would confirm the United States' status as a military and economic superpower.

The restored faith in America and its achievements under the Roosevelt administration was remarkable. Still, Roosevelt's legacy was not perfect: Truman could not simply slip into the presidency, close World War II, and return the nation to normalcy. Roosevelt's domestic and international dealings left many complications for which Truman had no answer.

> *"Most of the problems a president has to face have their roots in the past."*
> — Harry S. Truman

When Truman heard of the president's death and understood his new role as the chief executive, he released a statement to the press the following day: "When they told me yesterday what had happened, I felt like the moon, the stars, and all the planets had fallen on me."

President Truman would have to address problems that even the great Roosevelt appeared unable to resolve. One of the most prominent domestic problems left by the Roosevelt administration was the question of the New Deal. Once viewed as the saving grace of the nation, Roosevelt's economic movements during the Depression needed great reorganizing now that the war had produced such prosperity. Roosevelt's New Deal brought the government into close contact with business, regulating it to save it from further collapse. With the coming of World War II and the great demand for tanks, planes, and other wartime productions, however, many believed the economy could reset itself and no longer needed such firm guidance.

Roosevelt made no plans for such changes in

Harry Truman had been selected to run as Franklin Roosevelt's vice president in 1944. He was sworn in as president on April 12, 1945, after Roosevelt died in office. Unfortunately for Truman, Roosevelt had kept him in the dark about the most pressing issues concerning the presidency, including the future of the New Deal and the spread of communism, leaving Truman largely unprepared for the office.

economics. In fact, many argue that Roosevelt made no plans for the New Deal's long-term survival, and so the postwar politicians argued its fate. Many wanted New Deal policies expanded to extend its life. Others felt that the great New Deal might irritate businesses that now wanted a laissez-faire, or "hands-off," approach in which the government generally would not involve itself with business dealings. President Truman faced the fate Roosevelt's once beloved and flawless New Deal would play in the country's conversion from a booming war economy to postwar inflation and finally to peaceful stability.

Of greater concern and complexity than his domestic policies were Roosevelt's international politics. He may have successfully entered the United States in World War II and created the alliances with England and Russia, but his later dealings caused great complications in closing the war. Of particular significance was how the United States would deal with communist Russia, a World War II ally, after the war was over.

This complex question requires an understanding of the political forces involved. Developed by Karl Marx, communism is an economic system in which the government has extensive control over people's lives and industry so that all may share in a common good. This economic system is in direct contrast with capitalism, the system of free industry practiced by the United States. Marx believed communism would naturally spread across the world after an inevitable collapse of capitalism. By the early- to mid-1900s, however, communist thought moved more toward forcing this collapse and actively seeking the global spread of communism. Capitalist countries such as the United

States would clearly resist such efforts, so communist Russia and capitalist America would be in direct opposition once they had defeated their common World War II enemies.

In February 1945, when it became clear that the Allied forces would defeat Germany in the West, the leaders of the three great powers, Russia, England, and the United States, met at Yalta to discuss the fate of Germany and further plans concerning war with Japan in the East. Here President Roosevelt was criticized for compromising too much with the Russian leader, Joseph Stalin. The president was pushing for the Russians to become quickly involved with the war on Japan and may have sacrificed too much to secure this.

As a result of the conference at Yalta, the Allies decided that land, ports, and railroads in the Chinese land of Manchuria would be given to both the Chinese and the Russians after it was liberated. This was decided without consulting China. Second, the Soviet Union would keep the land in eastern Poland that it had occupied when fighting Germany. Third, the lands in Eastern Europe liberated from German occupation were to hold free elections.

These points made at the Yalta conference appeared to encourage the growth of communist Russia. The Russian presence in Manchuria alarmed many and offended China. When China became communist in 1949, many remembered Roosevelt having allowed the Russian influence to be so easily introduced. More crucial were the last two points. Roosevelt seemed to have only encouraged the

In February 1945, it became clear that the Axis Powers (Germany, Italy, and Japan) would lose World War II, and English Prime Minister Winston Churchill (left), President Roosevelt (center), and Russian leader Joseph Stalin (right) met in Yalta to discuss the future of Germany and the war in Japan. Truman would have to deal with the results of this conference, particularly in regard to Russian communism, during his presidency.

spread of communism by giving Russia eastern Poland. As for free elections, Roosevelt had no real reason to think that Stalin would ever keep his word on this. Everyone seemed to know that Russia would later betray the Yalta discussions and forcefully bring these countries into the Soviet Union without free elections.

Again, Roosevelt proved only to be helping the spread of communism. Truman would be forced to deal with this shortsightedness. The United States and Russia would become enemies after World War II, as the United States would compete for support of democratic capitalism to resist the global spread of communism. Roosevelt may have made Truman's struggle harder by allowing communism to spread easily into Eastern Europe and other parts of the world.

In addition to the specific problems with the New Deal and Yalta, Roosevelt complicated Truman's presidency by not taking the office of vice president seriously. The vice president traditionally holds minimal power outside his role as president of the Senate. Roosevelt, like many past presidents, cared little to have his vice president fully informed of all the country's dealings.

Even more dangerous was Roosevelt's secretive wartime nature. Truman did not attend any significant war discussions and scarcely knew of the major operations. He had only heard vague whispers of new scientific research in atomic weaponry. When Roosevelt died in April 1945, the war with Germany was not yet won and the Japanese front seemed far from over. Truman would assume the role of president with very basic knowledge of the war strategies and would be expected to successfully lead the United States through the rest of World War II.

Although Truman had no substantial hand in the planning of the war, country and military officials looked to him for decisions Roosevelt could have better prepared him to make. To prevent this problem from occurring again, Truman increased the involvement of the vice president in secret national affairs and made sure that the vice president attended more national security discussions.

THE BOMB

AFTER BEING SWORN in on April 13, 1945, Truman was approached by military advisors to discuss the remaining war efforts. It would be possible to close the war with Germany within months; however, the war with Japan would be far more complicated.

The advisors were unsure of how long the war in the East would last, especially with Japan's extensive island control. Although it was difficult to push Japanese forces out of all the islands they occupied, America had developed the "island hopping" technique in which U.S. forces would liberate the main island of a group and thus force the others to fall. This may have been effective, but it was also a very long process. It was estimated that the war might not end for another three or more years. Attacking mainland Japan would also be very risky. Japanese forces, especially the kamikaze, could make air strikes and land invasions close to impossible. The kamikaze, or suicide pilots, would fly their planes into enemy forces, and the explosions of their aircraft would cause heavy damage to naval units. President Truman had to consider all of this if the United States wished to begin planning a stronger attack on Japan after the close of the German front.

The president's briefing on the war would also have involved the report that American scientists were within months of completing a bomb of unprecedented destruction. On July 6, 1945, the plutonium test bomb "Trinity" was successfully detonated in Alamogordo, New Mexico. The president received word just in time for the Potsdam Conference of July 17 to August 2. Germany had surrendered on May 8, so the Allied Powers gathered once again, this time to discuss postwar Europe and the continuing battle in the East. With a successful test of an atom bomb, Truman could sit quite comfortably when dealing with Stalin.

The Potsdam Declaration of July 26 warned Japan that, like Germany, it would be forced into an "unconditional surrender." In this warning, Truman did not mention the new bomb that could vaporize entire cities, and Japan ridiculed what seemed like an absurd declaration. President Truman authorized the use of the atomic bomb on August 5, 1945, and the *Enola Gay*,

In late 1945, Churchill (left), Truman (center), and Stalin (right) met in Potsdam to discuss postwar Europe and the war in Japan, which was still in progress. Although the threat of communism spreading had become more intimidating since the Yalta Conference, Truman would act with new confidence when dealing with Russia at Potsdam, as word of the atomic bomb's successful testing reached the president only days before the conference.

the plane armed with the uranium bomb known as "Little Boy," left for the city of Hiroshima early the next day. Almost 90 percent of the city was leveled in the explosion, and between 70,000 and 130,000 people were killed. Japan, left in a state of shock, still hesitated to surrender. President Truman answered by authorizing the use of the plutonium bomb "Fat Man" on Nagasaki. This second bomb, which was dropped on August 9, killed approximately another 45,000 people. Truman received his unconditional surrender from Japan on August 14, 1945. The use of the atom bomb brought World War II to its close and changed modern warfare forever.

THE DEBATE

Truman's critics maintain that his use of the bomb was inhumane, unnecessary, and un-American. Since the dropping of the bombs, many people, Americans included, have thought that incinerating two cities and causing such severe civilian casualties violated the basic rules of war and humanity. People see not a weapon of war but one of mass murder. Critics say that two bombs of two different types of radioactive material (uranium and plutonium) on two untouched cities is problematic. It seems more like the United States military was using these cities and thousands of citizens to test the extent of destruction these new weapons of mass destruction could inflict. President Truman could have detonated a bomb on a remote location on Japanese soil to warn of the weapon's incredible force before deploying it on an unsuspecting city. Many feel that America, a country that claims to stand for the freedom and human rights of all, should never have engaged in such unprecedented mass destruction of innocent civilians, especially without warning.

Another criticism of Truman's action is that detonating the weapon might have been more about intimidating Russia than forcing Japan to surrender. Russia had been slow in moving its troops toward the East and joining the war against Japan When the power of the bomb presented itself, Truman would no longer need Soviet assistance and so could rush its use before Russia got involved. Russia joined the war soon after the bombings, but Japan surrendered within days. By detonating the nuclear weapons, President Truman could show Russia that the United States had a military of incredible power that it was not afraid to use.

America defeated Japan on its own with the use of this new weaponry, and the nation's power seemed limitless with such an arsenal. The power to level cities would certainly aid Truman in stopping the spread of communism throughout the world. In light of America's remarkable military demonstration, Russia might be more hesitant to ignore U.S. wishes and try to extend the communist reach. Critics find problems with this reasoning because although it may be politically advantageous, it also allows killing one country's citizens for the sake of intimidating another. People argue that even if Russia was impressed with American strength, Truman's destruction of the Japanese cities was not the best way to give such an impression.

Defenders of Truman's action insist that using the atomic bombs on the two cities was the only reasonable way to end the war. Truman did not simply order that the bombs be used as soon as he heard of their existence. He discussed the option with his top advisors, and they all agreed to using it because the Japanese showed no signs of surrender. Their suicide bombers and two million troops would resist to a bitter end. The battle for the island of Okinawa alone claimed 48,000 American lives, and the mainland might be much worse. The battles would be long and bloody, and Japanese atrocities would continue.

President Truman would claim that rushing the bombs was not to impress Russia but to save American lives and prevent further Japanese horrors, especially the brutality toward U.S. prisoners of war. In addition, when the first bomb leveled Hiroshima, Japan did not instantly call for peace. When the second was dropped, their vote to surrender was not overwhelming, and many Japanese officials still considered resisting. President Truman may have been justified in his claims that Japan would not surrender until the bitter end and that if the war progressed as anticipated, both sides could lose more than the combined number killed by the atomic bombs. For President Truman, the bombs were the only way to prevent the predicted years added to this already long and brutal war.

President Truman would also insist that his use of the bombs on cities resulted out of military necessity. It is important to note that President Truman had only two

Smoke from the first atomic bomb the United States dropped on the Japanese city of Hiroshima had spread out 10,000 feet when the smoke from the second bomb, which was dropped on Nagasaki four days later, rose in a thick column 20,000 feet in the air. Although Japan surrendered unconditionally on August 14, 1945, ending World War II, Truman's authorization to use the bomb was sharply criticized at the time and remains a point of controversy to this day.

bombs (which cost over $2 billion), and his advisors told him that they were unsure if they would even work. The president's choice of a city over a deserted warning site would avoid military embarrassment and setbacks in case the bomb did not detonate. Even if the test bomb worked,

34

there was no guarantee that the second bomb would detonate, and the United States would be left without any damage to Japan. Truman also believed that these cities were of great military importance to Japan and that destruction of them would cripple Japan's war effort.

Truman's desire to end the war remained constant, which is demonstrated by his support for the establishment of the United Nations (UN). Plans for a lasting organization composed mainly of the Allied powers of World War II began in 1943. After the war, President Truman, the leader of one of the two lasting superpowers, had a large influence on the fate of such an organization. Although the United Nations may have been

> "When Kansas and Colorado have a quarrel over the water in the Arkansas River they don't call out the National Guard in each state and go to war over it. They bring a suit in the Supreme Court of the United States and abide by the decision. There isn't any reason in the world why we cannot do that internationally."
>
> — Harry S. Truman

biased toward the West (European and American interests), the point remains that Truman had no need to establish a mechanism for ensuring lasting peace. He held one of the world's greatest militaries, the best production lines, and exclusive access to the most devastating weapon in the world (which he had deployed twice already). With such security and intimidation, Truman could easily have stalled the UN organization. However, his view that power, even in the awesome form of the atomic bomb, can be used to end wars and not begin them seems to be consistent with his support of the UN Charter.

Through his efforts, the council of countries met in San Francisco and drafted the charter, which was ratified on October 14, 1945, two months after the end of the war. Although not entirely his design, the UN is partially a Truman legacy, because his support helped ensure its establishment. Today, the UN consists of a much larger global community that funds peace initiatives around the world.

The debate over Truman's decision to use the atomic bomb continues to this day. In 1995, on the 50th anniversary of the attacks, Japan and the United States both contemplated apologizing to each other for Pearl Harbor and the atom bombs, respectively. Citizens from both countries were appalled at the idea, and the apologies never occurred. Because the idea of a nuclear weapon had never existed before this time, Truman had been placed in a position of great power—the decision ultimately came down to him, with no Congress, no courts, and no vote of the people to help him. In his memoirs, Truman recognized this and took full responsibility for his actions: "The final decision of where and when to use the bomb was up to me. Let there be no mistake about it."

> "All my life, whenever it comes time to make a decision, I make it and forget about it."
> — Harry S. Truman

Truman was decisive, but at the cost of thousands of civilians. Still, his decisiveness may have saved thousands more lives and brought a close to the bloodiest war in history. Of course, Truman, with his typical stubborn conviction, gave his opinion of those who challenged his decision in a 1959 talk with Columbia University students: "All this uproar about what we did and what could have been stopped—should we take these wonderful Monday morning quarterbacks, the experts who are supposed to be right? They don't know what they are talking about. I was there. I did it. I would do it again."

AFTER THE WAR

THE CLOSE OF World War II solidified the United States' position as a military superpower; however, the economic struggles of peacetime threatened the stability of everyday American life. The economic boom of the early 1940s resulted from the country's overwhelming demand for military supplies. The U.S. government generously contracted factories and businesses to supply the war effort, and the decade-long Great Depression was soon replaced with 100 percent employment and increased wages.

When the demand for workers and production materials of planes, tanks, and other supplies ended, the Truman administration was faced with converting the production of wartime

After World War II ended, Truman faced trying domestic problems, including the economic difficulties of adjusting to peacetime. He struggled to pass legislation through an uncooperative Congress, one controlled by his own party. This cartoon of Truman talking to Speaker of the House Sam Rayburn supposes Truman's feelings about the 1946 election, which resulted in a Republican Congress.

products to that of everyday, consumer products. Government war contracts would end, and if there was nothing to replace war production, businesses would fail and unemployment would again soar. Above all, Truman feared the postwar inflation that would follow such a large-scale war — with too much money in circulation from the wartime boom and too few non-war products available for purchase, the value of the dollar could significantly decrease.

With such potential for inflation and unemployment, many saw the end of World War II as a possible return of the Great Depression. Although Roosevelt's New Deal was quite innovative, many historians believe that only World War II can be credited with saving the United States from the Great Depression. Without the war, the economy would have crashed back to the unstoppable depression.

Still, New Dealers like Truman could certainly defend the program's results and resist the return of the Depression by continuing New Deal legislation. However, the capitalist economy, revived by the war, would not benefit from the government control inherent in New Deal programs but from a return to more laissez-faire economics. It appeared now that both saviors of the Depression, the war and the New Deal, would be removed; this dilemma weighed heavily on President Truman, who feared that the coming inflation echoed too strongly the start of another Great Depression.

Many of the Truman administration's attempts to stabilize the postwar economy were marked with failure. Within the first ten days of peace, almost two million Americans lost their jobs. In the year following World War II, millions more would lose their jobs, and there would be continual strikes in critical industries like steel, mining, and railroads.

Truman's problems began with his neglect to expand peace conversion plans during the war. Most of his attention went to winning the war, and so the country was not ready to handle the aftermath. When the war ended and Truman had begun to focus heavily on the inflation concerns, his ineffective appointees to powerful cabinet positions only furthered the administration's struggles.

The failures of his administration cannot lie solely on Truman. For the most part, the economic experts and advisors of the time simply had no idea how to deal with the problems of the postwar inflation. This uncertainty resulted in arguments, confusion, and poorly planned legislation. Truman also fought endlessly with Congress, which had become considerably less liberal since the height of the New Deal. The government was too

> "I am having the usual amount of trouble and bickering. When the Congress get all snarled up, it is necessary for them to find someone to blame—so they always pick on me."
>
> — Harry S. Truman

divided at a time when it needed to produce swift and powerful legislation. Whatever the cause of the problems, the people blamed their president—Truman's approval rating in the Gallup Poll dropped from 87 percent to 32 percent within the year-and-a-half following the war, and people saw a mediocre executive failing their expectations of America's greatness.

Truman's frustration with Congress during 1945 and 1946 centered mainly on government involvement in the economy and the issue of price controls. During the war, the government had implemented price ceilings on many goods to control the market price and keep goods affordable for consumers. However, these extensive price controls were in direct opposition of Congress and its wish to return to laissez-faire economics. The Democratic Party held the majority in Congress and is traditionally more in favor of price controls and government involvement. However, with the economic boom of World War II, many Democrats felt that there was no longer a need for such controlling legislation. Such was the case in the Democratic Congress of 1945–46.

STRIKES AND DOMESTIC CRISIS

Truman continued to support price controls and believed that they were the only way to stop "runaway inflation"—an unstoppable, seemingly limitless cycle in which inflation creates more inflation. Truman failed to persuade a Congress with a majority comprised of his own political party to maintain price controls at his proposed levels. Price controls continually expired until all were lifted by November 9, 1946. Whether or not the removal of price controls was effective is debatable; however, the frustration and inability of the president to enact his plans was quite clear. The American people were equally frustrated, and in November 1946, they elected the first Republican Congress since 1930.

These economic problems eventually resulted in widespread strikes. When striking, workers band together and refuse to work until the managers of the business meet their demands, which range from wage increases to improved working conditions. In theory, with the entire workforce gone, employers will listen to worker demands out of fear for losing the business. If there is no one in the production factory, the management and business people will have nothing to sell. The strike strategy was quite effective and led to the establishment of nationwide labor unions in which workers formally agreed to always act together—if only a few strike, management can easily replace the missing workers. In fact, the risk of striking comes with the possibility that management will just replace everyone.

During the post-World War II economic struggles, workers and management could never agree upon wages, and even when the president tried to mediate, compromises between the two sides failed. The labor unions of critical industries like steel and railroads were so powerful that they were able to implement crippling, nationwide strikes. Steelworkers went on strike in January 1946, coal miners on May 18 that year, and most importantly, rail workers on May 23. The early steel strike was resolved quickly, but as more strikes continued, the government's ability to smoothly settle them lessened. Enraged, Truman would watch private business almost destroy itself with disagreements between employers and employees.

Although these strikes occurred in the private business sector, or those businesses not owned by the "public" U.S. government, the federal government had to intervene: Without the steel and railroad industries, America's entire production and transportation networks would collapse.

Steelworkers joyfully burn their strike posters in the January cold after being notified that a new wage contract had been reached. In 1946 two other groups went on strike: coal miners on May 18 and railroad workers on May 23. Workers wanted better wages and could not agree with management. Truman used his power as president to seize the industries and place them under government control.

In times of emergency, the government has the right to seize such industries and run all of its functions. President Truman exercised such power. The threat of shutting down American railroads seemed more than substantial as an emergency, and President Truman soon ordered a federal seizure of the rail lines.

The president's sense of helplessness and anger peaked during this crisis. Despite government control of the railroads, there were no workers to run them, and the military could not easily learn the job to replace them. Even when he took action as president and seized the industry, Truman could do nothing to resolve the situation. At the height of his frustration, he asked Congress for the power to draft the workers directly into the military so he could order them back to work. Fortunately, the rail strike ended mid-speech, and this radical demand died with it.

President Truman seemed to be unable to bring about any substantial economic improvement during the postwar conversion period. Besides needing to address global political instability, Russian expansion and aggression, and the federal economic policies, the president had to baby-sit private business and resolve its

Truman's Anger

Truman developed a peculiar habit of writing scathing letters out of anger and frustration but never sending them. However, when Paul Hume, a music critic, provided less than favorable reviews of the vocal performance of Truman's daughter at a 1950 recital, Truman sent one of his letters to the critic: "Some day I hope to meet you. . . . When that happens you'll need a new nose, a lot of beefsteak for bad eyes, and perhaps a supporter below!" This created much controversy for the White House, because it seemed only to further confirm Truman's image as a frustrated, ill-tempered man unsuited for diplomatic delicacy.

internal problems. Truman certainly despaired during this period, and he was joined in this despair with the American people. Americans lost faith in their leader, perhaps feeling that great men like Roosevelt would surpass such challenges. In a famous memo to himself, Truman illustrated his anger with bickering laborers and a resistant Congress:

> . . . tell them [union leaders] that patience is exhausted. Declare an emergency—call out troops. Start industry and put everyone back to work who wants to go to work. If any leader interferes court martial him. . . . Adjourn Congress and run the country. Get plenty of atomic bombs on hand—drop one on Stalin, put the United Nations to work and eventually set up a free world.

The president's solutions, although humorous, are those of an overwhelmed, desperate man who sees that his only options are absurd and fantastical.

Expressing anti-Truman sentiment seemed to be the country's pastime. People continually joked that "To err is Truman," and by early 1947, some of his own advisors encouraged him to resign the presidency. Congress continued to resist him and had gathered enough strength to successfully override his veto of the Taft–Hartley Act on June 20, 1947. Drafted by Representative Fred A. Hartley and Senator Robert A. Taft, this important legislation reworked the National Labor Relations Act of

1935 and increased the president's power to counter the threat of union strikes. President Truman vetoed the bill in the hope of protecting labor interests, but the veto failed.

With the people and Congress so clearly against Truman, Republicans could finally consider a serious chance of controlling the White House after the 1948 elections. Truman's 36 percent approval rating in the April 1948 Gallup Poll seemed to solidify the eventual dismissal of a failed president.

5

TRUMAN'S TRIUMPH

POOR POLLS IN early 1947 and 1948 do not necessarily slate the entire year as a repeated failure of 1946. In fact, 1947 was much more productive for Truman, especially in the realm of foreign politics. The economy began to heal much on its own, and the internal economic pressure and frustration were released. Truman also made great progress in balancing the federal budget. The people responded with significant increases in his approval ratings for the year. Truman's successful international efforts with the Truman Doctrine and Marshall Plan directly contradicted the image of the bumbling domestic president who seemed incapable of taking significant action.

General George C. Marshall became Truman's secretary of state in 1947. At the time, there was concern Greece and Turkey would fall to communist influence. In a speech before Congress, Truman proposed offering aid to those countries in order to prevent the spread of communism, a policy known as the Truman Doctrine. Congress later approved a more developed form of this plan, known as the Marshall Plan after Secretary Marshall.

INTERNATIONAL GREATNESS

In early 1947, Truman brought great strength to his disorderly cabinet when he dismissed the incompetent James F. Byrnes and appointed General George C. Marshall as secretary of state. With a man of Marshall's excellent character, thought, and administrative efficiency in the most powerful cabinet seat, Truman was assured of the capability of his office to manage foreign affairs effectively in a time of such international importance.

Postwar Europe had been largely destroyed and fell quickly to continuing threats of widespread poverty and starvation. The weakened Europe was very susceptible to Russian influence, and Communist parties gained strength throughout the continent, most alarmingly in France and Italy, traditional keystones of Western strength.

Britain could no longer maintain its role as an international superpower and announced that it would remove its foreign aid from Greece and Turkey at the end of March 1947. All political analysts agreed that Greece and Turkey would certainly fall to communism if they received no foreign aid. The United States now stood at a crossroads: It could do nothing and maintain its avoidance of Europe and its problems, for which it had already suffered involvement in two bloody world wars, or it could position itself as a modern superpower —the most wealthy and powerful of the free world— that must defend this freedom against the persistent communist threat.

Truman, backed by Secretary Marshall's advice and support, decided to aid Greece and Turkey, and so initiated the cold war politics that would dominate the second half of twentieth-century American foreign policy. The executive administration believed that if Greece and Turkey fell to communism, all of the surrounding

Mediterranean countries would follow as falling dominoes ("domino theory"). Communism, and the Soviet aggression Truman linked to it, would spread through Europe and throughout the world until the United States itself would be subject to its attacks. The United States, although bitter from Europe's wars, could not afford isola-

> *"The absence of war is not peace."*
>
> — Harry S. Truman, on his belief that the United States could not remain idle, thinking that the world was "at peace" and allow the communist threat to grow

tionism and to allow the Soviet strength to grow beyond any possible future resistance.

Truman, who saw his country as the pillar of freedom, looked not just to the ultimate defense of his country but also to defense of freedom in the world. Truman believed this to be "right," and he would continually strive to act on his instinct for truth separate from personal interest, anger, or political corruption. This ideal was not always reached, but President Truman later became known for making decisions according to what he believed was "right" for his country and the free world.

These ideas may have seemed clear enough when discussed among Truman, Marshall, and the executive office, but the nation and its resistant Republican Congress would be a more difficult audience. Determined, Truman addressed the 80th Congress on March 12, 1947, with the Truman Doctrine—his proposal for granting Greece and Turkey $400 million in military and economic assistance. The president alluded to

Russian aggression, but never mentioned it by name, and made clear his vision of America as the protector of the free world:

> We shall not realize our objectives, however, unless we are willing to help free peoples to maintain their free institutions and their national integrity against aggressive movements that seek to impose upon them totalitarian regimes. This is no more than frank recognition that totalitarian regimes imposed upon free peoples, by direct or indirect aggression, undermine the foundations of international peace and hence the security of the United States. . . . The Government of the United States has made frequent protests against coercion and intimidation, in violation of the Yalta Agreement, in Poland, Rumania, and Bulgaria [i.e.: Russian coercion and intimidation]. . . . I believe that it must be the policy of the United States to support free peoples who are resisting attempted subjugation by armed minorities and outside pressures. I believe that we must assist free peoples to work out their own destiny in their own way. . . . The free peoples of the world look to us for support in maintaining their freedoms.

Congress approved the Truman Doctrine, Greece and Turkey received support, and the U.S. foreign policy of containment had begun. The president's speech referred not just to Greece and Turkey but also to worldwide freedom. Truman spoke of "direct or indirect" aggression, and so any perceived aggression, not just that of full war, might also warrant U.S. assistance. communist countries, seeking to spread their influence across the globe, would now find U.S. capital flowing to bordering countries to support their resistance and contain the aggression.

As an interesting side note, Truman seemed to refer only to Europe when he mentioned "world"—at least at this point in time—because China received no funding and fell to communism in 1949. Truman probably believed that American aid could do nothing substantial to prevent communism from reaching China. Still, the Western bias of his speech is evident.

With congressional approval of foreign support, Truman and Marshall naturally turned to their main concerns: the ruined seats of power in Western Europe—France, Italy, West Germany, and so on. Secretary Marshall's Harvard Commencement Speech was the springboard for the Marshall Plan, which ultimately proposed a bigger and better Truman Doctrine to Congress. Congress eventually approved the plan, and $17 billion found its way to Europe to assist postwar recovery, block communist influence, and secure the American interest of promoting capitalism in the name of freedom. The eventual recovery of Western Europe is credited primarily to the successful efforts of President Truman and Secretary Marshall.

Truman's international political success continued into 1948, when he laid the foundation for the organization of the North Atlantic Trade Organization (NATO). In

PRESIDENT TRUMAN'S LEGACY

Containment

President Truman's foreign affairs policies shaped the remaining half of the twentieth century. Successfully closing World War II and armed with nuclear weaponry he was ready to use, President Truman led the United States through its initial growth into a modern superpower.

Many historians credit President Truman for saving postwar Europe. His initiatives with the Truman Doctrine and the Marshall Plan bought the financial support needed to restart the Western economies. His provisions for American aid not only rebuilt Europe but also helped it resist the communist threat pressing against its borders. Truman's containment policy proved to be successful, as communism never fully penetrated the German divide into the core countries of France, Italy, or England. Further securing global containment, Truman forged the NATO alliance, which continues to operate as one of the most effective global organizations.

Truman expanded his containment policy both internally and abroad. He formed new alliances with Eastern countries to further tighten the free world's defense networks. Assisting South Korea in repelling the Northern invasion, Truman set the American policy of directly securing the free world against forced communism. His ordering and future support of NSC-68 bought the United States increased nuclear weapons and its largest standing peacetime military.

In essence, Truman prepared the country and the world for what he believed was the inevitable confrontation with Russia and communism. Critics note how Truman's aggressive containment policy may have forced Russia and the United States into entering the cold war. Still, if, as he predicted, the confrontation was unavoidable, Truman successfully secured the United States' ability to effectively shape world politics and resist the growing Russian power.

response to an alliance called "The Warsaw Pact" formed by Russia and various communist countries, President Truman sought to organize an alliance of The United States, Canada, and European powers to promote the security of capitalist interests and its free world. On April 4, 1949, the NATO alliance formed and Belgium, Canada, Denmark, France, Great Britain, Iceland, Italy, Luxembourg, the Netherlands, Norway, Portugal, and the United States agreed to collective self-defense (under Article 51 of the United Nations Charter): An attack against one would be an attack on all.

For the remainder of the century, European countries continued to enter the alliance, including Greece (1952), Turkey (1952), West Germany (1955), Spain (1982), and the Czech Republic, Hungary, and Poland (1999). This alliance formed one of the most effective containment devices for the free world and has been quite powerful and stabilizing in other ways throughout its existence. NATO, with 18 allied countries and headquarters in Brussels, Belgium, continues to operate and remains one of Truman's greatest legacies. With the fall of the Soviet Union, even Russian satellite countries sought NATO involvement. Twenty-seven countries signed a "Partnership for Peace" in 1994, although they are not all bound to the strict collective defense of the core NATO countries.

Truman also handled the Russian blockade crisis in Berlin effectively. After the war, Germany was split into Eastern and Western zones of control. Half of Berlin was controlled by Russia, and the other half was divided

Children in West Berlin watch as U.S. planes bring supplies into the blockaded city. The Russians formed the blockade along the border of East and West Germany on June 24, 1948. The blockade was intended to halt supplies from entering the western half and thus force it under the control of the East. Two days later, Truman authorized airlifts of supplies to West Germany, which lasted for 11 months.

among the three Western powers: England, France, and the United States. On June 24, 1948, Russia formed a blockade along the border that threatened to cripple the supplies to the Western zones of control and force the entire city to fall into the East. The crisis seemed as if it would end with either the fall of Berlin or conflict with Russia.

Two days later, Truman opted to begin a risky airlift of supplies above the blockade that ultimately saved the western part of the city. Just as Russia would argue that it could rightfully set up a blockade along its controlled border, so the British and American airlift allies could argue for their right to use the sky over Germany. Truman's avoidance of direct conflict proved successful when, on May 12, 1949, the Soviets ended their failed blockade. The Berlin Airlift officially ended on September 30.

TRUMAN IGNORED

With such a series of successes as the Truman Doctrine, Marshall Plan, early NATO initiatives, and the Berlin airlift campaign, it seemed that the Truman administration had organized itself and improved its ability to effect action since the embarrassments of 1946. Still, the Gallup Poll's 36 percent approval rate remained, and the poor ratings continued into the middle of the election year. The improved ratings of 1947 had

> *"The buck stops here."*
> — Harry S. Truman, on a sign placed on his desk to remind himself and others of executive responsibility. A twist on the phrase "pass the buck," it describes how the major actions and decisions come down to the president

disappeared, and it seemed that Truman might only have been riding the healing economy—once people began to consider reelection in 1948, they no longer cared for their mediocre president. He appeared to have done nothing actively important to the economy and bitterness returned.

Perhaps Americans failed to understand the great foundations Truman forged for United States politics until years after, when the recovery of Europe and the NATO alliance fully manifested themselves. Also, many anti-Semitic Americans were bitter over his recognition of Israel's nationhood (May 14, 1948), and others were simply unimpressed at how poorly communicated and unorganized this recognition was.

Whatever the case, the America of early 1948 sent clear signals that its executive office would change. Despite resistance from the public and his own his party, stubborn Truman, with unfinished work, announced he would "give 'em hell" and run for reelection on March 8, 1948.

The Democratic Party was not pleased with this decision. Like the rest of the country, the party felt that Truman had no substantial chance for reelection, so they looked to other possible candidates.

Many wanted Dwight D. Eisenhower to run for the Democrats, but he eventually declined the offer (he became president as a Republican in 1952). Even with Eisenhower down, Truman had to compete with Strom Thurmond of the Dixiecrats and Henry Wallace of the Progressives. The Dixiecrats, based in the American South, despised Truman's liberal civil rights programs, and the Progressives found Truman too conservative, especially with labor issues. Simply winning the Democratic nomination would not be sufficient, because these two men would run for president as independents and split the Democratic votes. The Democrats of the country would vote among three candidates and the Republicans could concentrate on their single presidential candidate, Thomas Dewey. Although his approval polls may have increased, Truman still faced the poor statistics of practical voting.

On September 18, seemingly against all odds, the hardworking, steadfast Truman began his infamous "whistle-stop" campaign throughout the country. He traveled all day by train, delivering speeches off the rear car platform at countless stops. He blamed the "do nothing" 80th Congress for all the failures of the people's expectations. This argument was quite strong considering Truman's brilliant move to call a special session of Congress to display its inability.

The Republican Party presented itself as somewhat liberal on certain issues to gain favor with the people and make Truman seem even more useless—a man unable to work with a cooperative Congress that agreed with some of his Democratic views. Truman put the Republican Congress to the test and called a special session to have it prove its somewhat liberal cooperation. The Congress did nothing. The president took this evidence, along with his determination to once again serve the nation, directly to the people surrounding each stop of his train platform.

Truman averaged a remarkable ten speeches a day and focused heavily on the Midwest. Dewey, his Republican opponent, avoided heavy campaigning, because most predicted he would win the election as long as he avoided any major mistakes. Less campaigning meant fewer chances for such blunders, and Dewey would simply coast his way into the White House. Truman's campaign perhaps dispelled much of the resentment that would allow Dewey such an easy victory. With his "whistle-stop" campaign, Truman appeared aggressive and in control, an image in direct opposition to the bumblings of 1946.

Truman's determination bought him a victorious election. The people seemed stunned by their own election, and Truman delighted in his own copy of the *Chicago Daily Tribune's* election newspaper, which assumed his defeat and went to press with headline "Dewey Defeats Truman" before the election results were final. The election turned in the Midwest, and many historians believe that the farmers feared and outvoted Republicans. Others note that Truman, who supported New Deal politics in his campaigning, relied also on the remaining Roosevelt coalition (the pool of voters President Roosevelt had firmly established).

Whatever the case, Truman pulled enough western states to steal the close election. Although Truman received 303 electoral college votes and Dewey only 189 (Thurmond received 39 and Wallace did not win any), states holding large electoral numbers sided in favor of Truman only slightly. Historian Roy Jenkins notes, "In a poll of nearly 50 million, a well distributed shift of 29,000 votes, just over .05 per cent of the total, could have produced a reversal."

Truman's approval ratings had fallen so drastically after the war that his defeat in the 1948 presidential election was practically assumed. Most of the country was surprised by Truman's win over Thomas Dewey, and the *Chicago Daily Tribune* even printed a headline proclaiming Dewey's victory before the election results were finalized.

President Truman triumphed, now elected to the office and no longer an accident of Roosevelt's death. The people also granted him a Democratic Congress and made clear their restored faith that he could guide America through the nation's rising greatness.

6

FAIR DEAL

PRESIDENT TRUMAN APPROACHED his next term with renewed confidence and hoped to enact his own version of New Deal politics, the Fair Deal, which focused heavily on social reform. He retained most of his trusted cabinet, and although George Marshall had to resign his position for health problems, Truman appointed the equally impressive Dean Acheson as secretary of state.

The president believed that the government owed its people a "Fair Deal" with which it could provide direct relief services and soften the brutal competition of raw capitalism. This traditionally liberal, and therefore Democratic, view assumes that capitalism

For his second term as president, Truman retained most of his cabinet. Dean Acheson (right) became secretary of state after George C. Marshall resigned because of health problems. Truman focused on social reform with the Fair Deal, his version of Roosevelt's New Deal.

needs close governmental supervision to prevent the helpless poor from being abused by the rich and powerful. Conservatives, usually associated with the Republican Party, side more with a purer form of capitalism in which the government is involved as little as possible—

capitalism and free economy form the perfect environment for the growth of business. Democrats feel that too much free capitalism cripples the poor, common citizen, and Republicans feel that too little cripples business and the great American economy.

With the liberal Fair Deal, Truman pushed for increased government programs to provide improved housing, healthcare, working conditions, social security, and civil rights for all Americans, and with the election of a Democratic Congress, the prospects of the Fair Deal appeared hopeful. However, as was the case in 1946, political party lines do not always fall clearly "conservative" or "liberal," and the 81st Congress of 1948–1950, although Democratic, possessed a strong conservative strain.

Unwilling to raise taxes to fund the proposed government programs of the Fair Deal, Congress blocked much of its legislation. When Congress did raise money, the funding only trickled into the Fair Deal. Congress also generally avoided the Fair Deal's liberal programs of increased government presence in daily American life. The result made Truman once again frustrated with domestic politics, making him unable to make any significant gains toward his Fair Deal objectives. He lost his fight for a national healthcare system to help people

"Whenever you have an efficient government you have a dictatorship."
— Harry S. Truman, revealing his respect for the democratic model of government of the United States despite his frustration with Congress

afford outrageous medical bills. Congress also blocked his agricultural plans to assist farmers.

In the interest of business, Congress refused Truman's request to repeal the Taft–Hartley Act. Truman originally vetoed the act in order to protect the power of common workers and their labor unions from abusive employers. A repeal of the act would reduce the government's power to control union strength, and after the strikes of previous years, Congress remained determined to let the act stand as law. Truman again lost with Congress, but Congress' insistence on Taft–Hartley beyond his veto and repeal request worked in Truman's favor. Historian Donald R. McCoy notes that Truman received the support of workers and labor unions by resisting the act but that he also benefited from using the powers the act granted him as president.

Problems began stirring in steel, coal, railroads, and other industries in late 1949 and early 1950. By June 1950, the railroad workers had gone on strike. President Truman turned his defeated veto to his advantage by controlling the labor situation with Taft–Hartley powers. He prevented many potentially disastrous situations and forced labor and management to smooth their differences in a more controlled manner. Only the railroads, which Truman seized until May 1952, required drastic measures.

Congress did not block every aspect of the Fair Deal, and Truman successfully pushed for his legislation whenever a window opened. As a result of Truman's efforts, the minimum wage program and antitrust legislation (laws against the formation of large, monopoly companies) increased to the benefit of laborers. Social security and development of affordable housing also expanded, and some provisions were made to keep energy and natural resources cheap and available. Still, President Truman found that these were minimal gains, because Congress would always cut either the funding or strength of these proposals. Truman wanted even more housing, social security, and so on, but Congress continually revised his goals—what became law always fell well short of Truman's vision.

CIVIL RIGHTS

Of important note is President Truman's inclusion of civil rights in his Fair Deal. President Truman included minorities when he spoke of "Americans" and those entitled to a Fair Deal. He recognized the contradiction of declaring such a deal while rampant discrimination of American minorities continued. The president's civil rights objectives, although perhaps small by modern standards, were quite significant and remain an arguable precursor to the major civil rights legislation of the 1960s. For the first time in the country's history, its president approached Congress with civil rights proposals: "We cannot be satisfied until all our people have equal opportunities for jobs, for homes, for education, for health, and for political expression, and until all our people have equal protection under the law." He outlined his controversial goals in 1948, even before his second term election, and continued to support them throughout his future Fair Deal politics.

Truman tried to effect as much improvement as possible. He asked for more anti-discrimination legislation, an end to lynching practices, and the removal of the poll tax. Although a poll tax, a fee charged to all voters, seems to affect everyone equally, it drastically hinders the poor from voting. Because most minorities, especially blacks, were locked into poverty by racist laws and conditions, they could not afford the poll tax and therefore could not vote to end the discrimination that crippled them. Like most forms of legally acceptable racism (often referred to as "institutionalized racism"), the system was cyclical and impossible to escape. Truman hoped to

PRESIDENT TRUMAN'S LEGACY

Fair Deal

Although Congress resisted legislation of the social reforms proposed in Truman's Fair Deal, they influenced future administrations. Truman's desire to increase medical, housing, and employee benefits slowly settled in the American consciousness. The extensive health care and social security networks that later developed have their roots in the Fair Deal.

Truman's Fair Deal vision also extended to minorities and the global community. His bold proposals laid the foundation for future presidents to address Congress with racial issues. Much of the 1960s civil rights movement has faint origin in Truman's intended policies. Truman also wanted to bring a better life to the underdeveloped countries of the world. His "Point Four" proposal began the major American policy of foreign assistance to the third world.

begin the work toward breaking these systems and to ensure that the Constitution applied to all citizens.

Again, Congress resisted the president's efforts. Predictably, the greatest—but not the only—dispute came from Southern states. Of particular irritation to Truman was the Senate's continued filibustering. While debating whether to vote a bill into law, Senators hold the right to speak for as long as they wish. Senators can thus "filibuster," or speak indefinitely, even reading from the local newspaper if they want to, and successfully block the official voting of the bill. Truman's administration tried to curb filibustering but instead found it further increased.

With such powerful resistance, Truman's civil rights legislation passed mostly in minimal forms. The president forged his own minor victories outside of Congress, appointing minorities to government positions and racially integrating the inaugural festivities of 1949.

Perhaps the most significant of Truman's actual gains came with his efforts to end military segregation. Minority military platoons were not supplied equally; nor were they treated with similar priority to those of whites. The contradiction in this area becomes painfully absurd—minorities were reminded even on the battle-field that the country for which they fought cared little in return for their respect and protection. On July 26, 1948, President Truman issued Executive Order 9981 (EO 9981) to racially integrate the U.S. military. EO 9981

Racial discrimination was one of the social problems that Truman worked to resolve during his second term. He wanted to end lynching, military segregation, and the poll tax, which prevented many poorer people, often minorities, from voting. Congress was again uncooperative: Only minimal civil rights legislation was passed.

established the President's Committee on Equality of Treatment and Opportunity in the Armed Services (also known as the "Fahy Committee," after its chairperson, Charles Fahy).

With the help of committee reports, the president

made significant advances toward integrating the air force, navy, and armed services throughout his following Fair Deal years. Historians George M. Elsey and Kweisi Mfume note that by nature of an executive order and the president's military authority, the resistant Congress was conveniently circumvented: "For future black service-men and -women, Executive Order 9981 represented a monumental step forward that never would have occurred if President Truman had sought the approval of the Eightieth Congress."

President Truman's Fair Deal fell far short of his expectations under the 81st Congress of 1948–1950. The Korean War in mid-1950 assured the continued underpinning of the Fair Deal for the remainder of his presidential term. Congress and the American people cared more for military and defense programs than for those of social welfare. It is the Fair Deal's vision that proved most significant, extending its value of civil rights and social welfare to future administrations. Where Truman failed to enact, he at least enabled.

As an almost unbelievable addendum to his Fair Deal to Americans, Truman took initiatives to also extend the right to a "fair deal" beyond American borders. In his 1949 State of the Union Address to Congress, Truman listed his four foreign policy objectives. "Point Four" (as it was later called) pushed beyond the scope of assisting Europe and other countries for the sake of containing communism. American aid should now extend to underdeveloped ("third world") countries throughout the world for the sake of humanitarian, not solely political, obligation. Truman believed that his Fair Deal extended from the same basic human rights that the Constitution references. Small wonder that when Americans even casually refer to their constitutional rights and privileges, they strongly echo those detailed and expanded in Truman's Fair Deal.

7

THE RISING
RED SCARE

OCTOBER 1949 DRASTICALLY changed the U.S. perspective of
the communist threat. On October 1, China officially declared
itself the "People's Republic of China." Communist leader Mao
Tse-Tung's communist forces had won the Chinese civil war and
pushed the U.S. favored Chiang Kai-Shek off the mainland to
the island of Formosa (now Taiwan). The United States and the
biased UN continued to recognize Chiang Kai-Sheik and Taiwan
as China's UN representative. Although formally convenient, this
could not soften the blow that communism had succeeded in
spreading to the world's most populated country. Later the same
month, Russia successfully detonated its own atomic bomb, and the

United States lost its comfortable monopoly on nuclear weapons. With the fall of China and the development of the Soviet bomb, Russian and communist power quickly reached alarming heights.

Exploiting this fear of the communist threat, an obscure senator, Joseph McCarthy, brought himself fame with his infamous "Red Scare" (red is the traditionally communist or Soviet color). A member of the Senate (representing Wisconsin), McCarthy endangered or destroyed the reputations of many U.S. government officials by accusing them of supporting communist and Russian agendas. He manipulated America's rising fear of communism to his own political end as he made these damaging accusations freely with little or no evidence.

Similar to the Salem witch trials in colonial Massachusetts, in which people were executed on the basis of rumor, McCarthy's indictments are often referred to as "witch-hunts." His attacks began with his speech on February 9, 1950 in Wheeling, West Virginia, as he unjustly charged Secretary Dean Acheson of allowing over a hundred communists in the State Department. The American people were terrified, investigations were ordered, and McCarthy increased his unfounded accusations. His "Red Scare" reached its peak under President Eisenhower's administration and lasted until December 2, 1954, when the U.S. Senate officially condemned his abuse of senatorial power.

McCarthy's witch-hunts, combined with increased

communist power in Russia and China, only furthered the cold war tensions between America and the Soviet Union under President Truman's administration. This tension would push to extremes over Korea, where the first "hot war" took place. Although the United States and Russia never declared war nor took direct military action on each other during the cold war, they fought indirectly by warring with armies of countries politically related to the opponent. These "hot wars" would bring the two countries dangerously close to an open war that could have resulted in World War III.

THE KOREAN WAR

With the Japanese surrender on August 15, 1945, Korea became a liberated country. American and Soviet forces quickly established opposite zones of occupation throughout the country, with the Soviets above the 38th parallel (38° north latitude) and U.S. forces below. Neither the United States nor Russia wanted to withdraw its influence for fear the other would see to the unification of Korea solely under communism or capitalism. Although many Koreans hoped for the country's unification, the occupying superpowers could not agree on combined North and South elections. By May 1948, the United States and the UN authorized free elections in the South alone, and the Republic of Korea, led by Syngman Rhee, was formed on August 15. The North soon followed with its own elections, forming the Democratic People's Republic of Korea on September 9 with Kim Il Sung as president.

Korea was liberated when Japan surrendered at the end of World War II. Opposing zones of occupation, one Russian and one American, were established. The Communist Russian forces took the land above the 38th parallel, which became known as North Korea. Free elections were held in South Korea in 1948, leading to the formation of the Republic of Korea under the leadership of Syngman Rhee.

Tensions between communist North and capitalist South continued to escalate until finally, on June 25, 1950, North Korea invaded the South. North Korea, partially equipped by the Russians and already the more industrialized of the two Koreas, could easily unite the country under communism. When word of the invasion reached Truman, the president needed to quickly decide whether to authorize the U.S. military to repel the Northern forces. The Korean debate significantly raised the stakes of Truman's containment policy, because now it would involve the direct use of the U.S. military.

Truman wanted to intervene, and in an attempt to gain international support, Secretary Acheson called the UN into session to decide the issue. Acheson was justified, and the UN voted to deploy its forces to assist South Korea under the direction of the United States (Russia refused to attend and so, conveniently, did not vote). Although the Korean War technically ran as a UN operation, the United States sent the majority of troops and controlled all military actions. With UN approval, President Truman immediately ordered U.S. forces to South Korea without fully consulting Congress.

Truman's decisiveness and speedy action perhaps saved the entire war effort. When U.S. forces reached South Korea in early July, the North Korean army had already captured the capital and stretched throughout almost the entire country. If totally controlled by North Korea, the Korean peninsula would have proven significantly more difficult for the landing of U.S. troops.

Although Truman's speedy action benefited the war effort, his avoidance of Congress was questionable. Article I, Section 8 of the United States Constitution reads "The Congress shall have Power . . . To declare War . . ." Although Truman claimed to act under executive authority that allowed him to send troops, he stretched this authority to the point of doing everything but officially declaring war. Congress received formal notification in mid-July, and an official war declaration followed. Truman set a powerful, controversial precedent in which the president could tread dangerously close to circumventing Congress's right to declare war.

MACARTHUR

General Douglas MacArthur, the war hero who headed U.S. forces in the Pacific front of World War II, held full command over the Korean operation. Upon entering nearly defeated South Korea, General MacArthur established and held a strong defensive line. He then launched his own offensive and reclaimed the capital city of Seoul on September 26. With the president's approval, MacArthur continued moving north, past the 38th parallel. His pace quickened as he became more confident, and he assured Truman that he need not worry about communist China's intervention on behalf of North Korea. Truman still advised caution and a slower pace, and MacArthur responded by splitting the army's forces to push faster toward the Yalu River border. On October 19, the United States

The tension between North Korea and South Korea soon escalated into a war. General Douglas MacArthur (right, with Truman) commanded the American forces in the Korean War. Truman and MacArthur disagreed often about the pace of the war and over the use of nuclear weapons against the communist Chinese forces. MacArthur was ultimately dismissed for insubordination.

captured the North Korean capitol of Pyongyang, and by November, only the uppermost northern region remained.

On November 26, Chinese forces crossed the Yalu River and helped the North Korean Army push back American forces. China, with such an enormous population, easily supplied a large military offensive. Its communist government also allowed for these large infantry numbers, because the government already had the authority to control its citizens in the interest of the "common good." Although poorly equipped in comparison to the Americans, the great number of Chinese troops was overwhelming. American soldiers in Korea later gave descriptions of firing their guns until the guns overheated and still seeing Chinese forces advancing.

The Chinese and North Koreans eventually pushed UN forces below the 38th parallel and recaptured Seoul in January 1951. On March 23, UN forces liberated Seoul again and pushed toward the 38th parallel. For the remainder of the war, the lines remained close to the 38th parallel, as neither side could make significant advances.

MacArthur became impatient during this stalemate. He asked the president for authorization to use nuclear weapons, but Truman denied his request. President Truman was already irritated with MacArthur, who, in adding ridiculous ultimatums to the Chinese, ruined the chance of an early cease-fire in March 1951. Nuclear authority would remain solely with the president and certainly not in MacArthur's anxious hands. MacArthur further irritated the situation by openly discussing the nuclear alternatives. Although Truman never intended to use the bomb, the talk of the subject led to misinterpretations and confusion that greatly alarmed the rest of the world. MacArthur's bad politics continued with his persistent public requests to attack China despite the world's and the United States' conviction to limit the war to Korea.

MacArthur's blatant insubordination finally forced Truman to dismiss the general on April 10, 1951. Truman's decision, although perhaps justified, was quite bold and controversial. People sympathized with the general and believed that his dismissal was too extreme. Truman, however, cared little for delicate treatment of a military officer's insubordination to his commander in chief. MacArthur returned to the United States with a grand welcome and a speech to Congress. Despite his political aspirations, he eventually fell into obscurity and died in 1964.

> "If there is one basic element of the Constitution, it is civilian control of the military. Policies are to be made by the elected political officials, not by generals or admirals."
>
> — Harry S. Truman, reflecting in his memoirs on the MacArthur incident

HEATING THE COLD WAR

The Korean War lingered on without any major offensives until an armistice was finally signed on July 27, 1953, under President Eisenhower. Casualties amounted to approximately 54,000 for the United States and one million for China. Korea, the most devastated, suffered the loss of three million people and extensive damage to its cities and countryside. To this day, Korea remains separated with a communist North and capitalist South.

Truman's decisiveness in entering the war demonstrated to the world the United States' belief in its containment policy. Beyond funding and supplies, the United States would risk engaging its military to combat any perceived communist aggression. Truman's entrance into the war also solidified the U.S. military as a device of diplomatic pressure. To combat the growing strength of the Soviet Union and communist forces, America could not maintain its skeletal isolationist army. The peacetime military needed to forever expand to ensure the proper defense of the nation and the free world.

President Truman also sought to expand the military defenses of free nations throughout the world. In 1951, Truman significantly increased his effort to strengthen free world alliances against communism. To assist the formation of these alliances, the president pushed for increased aid to weaker nations. In October, Congress passed the Mutual Security Act and authorized $6.9 billion in international funding. Truman secured NATO cooperation while also expanding the scope of containment to the Pacific and Middle East. Although he found little success in the Middle East, Truman had established Pacific alliances among Australia, New Zealand, and the United States (ANZUS) by April 1952. He was also able to forge alliances with Japan and surrounding countries and further strengthen Pacific resistance to communism.

Truman also aided a famine in India during the early 1950s in order to secure its stability against communism. With all his aggressive attention to those countries vulnerable to the communist threat, Truman effectively began an expanded international containment policy that further tightened around Russian interests.

Many historians criticize the president's hesitance to act more peacefully toward Russia. If he had been more concerned with speaking with the Russians instead of racing to arm the free world with economic and military aid, perhaps the almost four-decade-long cold war could have been avoided. Still, President Truman felt that he had made enough gestures to Russia and that it was Russia that was unwilling to settle differences. Whatever his reasoning, Truman believed that Russian and Communist aggression would never gently end and that the United States would have to arm itself and the remaining free world to effectively stop its global spread.

In early 1950, Truman had already begun to compare U.S. and Russian military size and capabilities. Sensing inevitable conflict and the need to protect the nation, he ordered an intense assessment of U.S. military strength compared to that of Russia's. The appointed committee produced the secret document, the National Security Council Memorandum Number 68 (NSC-68). The memorandum depicts the weakness of the United States' non-nuclear forces and insists on their strengthening. NSC-68 also pushed for further development of the devastating thermonuclear bomb, or hydrogen bomb ("H Bomb"), to counter the Soviets' certain development of such a weapon. Ultimately, NSC-68 required a military buildup priced at $50–$60 billion. With the expanding communist threat, the United States could no longer look to a small, peaceful army. NSC-68 reads:

> There are some who advocate a deliberate decision to isolate ourselves. . . . This argument overlooks the relativity of capabilities. With the United States in an isolated position, we would have to face the probability that the Soviet Union would quickly dominate most of Eurasia, probably without meeting armed resistance. It would thus acquire a potential far superior to our own, and would promptly proceed to develop this potential with the purpose of eliminating our power, which would, even in isolation, remain as a challenge to it and as an obstacle to imposition its order in the world [i.e., Communism]. There is no way to make ourselves inoffensive to the Kremlin [the government headquarters in Moscow] except by complete submission to its will [Russia will not accept peaceful relations with the U.S. even if it remains isolated—it will seek war until the U.S. surrenders to Communism]. Therefore isolation would in the end condemn us to capitulate or to fight alone and on the defensive, with drastically limited offensive and retaliatory capabilities in comparison with the Soviet Union.

After reviewing NSC-68 in early 1950, the members of the Truman administration knew that the proposals would encounter extreme resistance in the Congress, because they would require a large tax increase. Truman's direct military involvement in Korea demonstrated the need for U.S. foreign policy to shift away from isolationism. The United States now certainly required a strong military in order to be taken seriously by Russia and to resist further communist aggression in the free world.

NSC-68 received its $50 billion budget as a direct result of the Korean War. Under Truman, the United States began building its largest peacetime army in history. Russia responded in a similar fashion. By 1952, U.S. scientists discovered the thermonuclear bomb, and Russian scientists followed the next year. The cold war thus came into full being, and the United States and Russia would continue to aggressively arm and counter-arm themselves for almost half a century.

AN UNEVENTFUL YEAR

The year 1952 was largely uneventful for the Truman administration. In foreign affairs, Truman continued his efforts to contain communism as the Korean War dragged on with poor negotiations. Outside the Korean War and the efforts to increase alliances, nothing of major inter-national significance occurred. The uneventful tension of the cold war began to take hold. Domestically, it became clear that Congress would continue its resistance of Truman and his Fair Deal plans for health care, education, civil rights, and so on.

Although the president did make some gains with

The Korean War officially ended with an armistice signed on July 27, 1953. The United States lost 54,000 lives, and China lost one million. Korea lost three million people and suffered devastation of its property, as this picture of a village in the Andong-Yechon area illustrates.

amendments to the Social Security Act, which benefited workers and the elderly, he again fell short of his overall Fair Deal expectations. Civil Rights and minority benefits were also silenced, although Puerto Rico did achieve self-government as a U.S. territory in 1952. The ongoing Korean War and increased communist threat made national defense programs the country's main interest, and Truman's Fair Deal fell even further from sight. When the Fair Deal did receive attention, Congress followed its trend of continually frustrating the president with resistance.

One crisis Truman faced in 1952 was the steel strike on April 9. In the interest of the labor workers, Truman refused to use the powers granted to him by Taft–Hartley Act and eventually just seized the steel mills to hopefully secure better benefits for the workers. However, in the *Youngstown v. Sawyer* case, the Supreme Court ruled that only Congress, not the president, had the power to seize private business The steel mills were returned to the private sector, and Congress asked Truman to enact his Taft–Hartley powers to stop striking laborers. Truman refused and instead requested that the government be able to seize the steel industry, which Congress then refused.

Assassination Attempt

Griselio Torresola and Oscar Collazo, two Puerto Rican Nationalists seeking to further the cause of Puerto Rican independence from the United States, attempted to shoot their way through the Blair House in Washington, D.C., where the Truman family was staying while the White House was being renovated. On November 1, 1950, Torresola and Collazo approached the Blair House and opened fire, hoping to assassinate the president in an effort to draw attention to their cause. A gun battle ensued between the policemen and secret service agents that were guarding the house and the two Nationalists. Torresola and one policeman were killed. President Truman was napping when the attempt took place and is said to have run to the window to discover the source of commotion. Noting the absurdity of a president curiously rushing toward gunfire, his guards quickly instructed him to move away.

Collazo was sentenced to death in 1951. Truman later reduced this sentence to life imprisonment, and President Jimmy Carter granted him a full pardon in 1979.

Fortunately, steel management and workers made an independent agreement and resolved the strike. The entire ordeal only further illustrated the inability of the president and Congress to agree on domestic policy.

Truman never seemed truly willing to run for reelection in 1952, and he finally declared that he would not be the presidential candidate for the Democratic Party. The democrats nominated Adlai Stevenson, and Truman supported him with extensive trips and speeches throughout the country. His campaigning for the Democratic Party had little effect, and the Republican nominee, Dwight D. Eisenhower, was elected president in November.

Although displeased with the Democratic loss, President Truman handled the transfer of power rather well. He set a new precedent when he invited President-Elect Eisenhower to the White House to discuss the transition. On January 20, 1953, President Dwight D. Eisenhower was sworn into office, and Harry S. Truman, after serving almost eight full years as the nation's president, soon left for his home in Independence, Missouri.

After leaving the presidential office at age 68, Truman lived for almost 20 more years. He avoided holding any further public positions, although he would openly endorse or oppose various political candidates and actions. During the early years of his presidential retirement, he worked primarily for the publication of his memoirs, entitled *Year of Decisions* (1955) and *Years of Trial and Hope* (1956).

Harry Truman did not hold any political offices after leaving the presidency, but he did endorse other candidates and make public appearances, such as this one on September 3, 1959 at the Truman Library in Independence, Missouri. Here, Truman plays a duet with Jack Benny, a popular performer of the 1950s.

On July 6, 1957, Truman achieved his greatest post-presidential success with the opening of the Harry S. Truman Museum and Library in Independence, Missouri. Truman had worked diligently to acquire sponsor support, and the library was built entirely from private funding. Although the library naturally focuses on President Truman's life, he also insisted that it tribute the presidential or executive office more generally. Truman placed his own personal office in the library and spent the remainder of his life maintaining the museum's celebration of the presidency. Future presidents visited Truman at the library and sometimes honored him by signing significant legislature in his presence. After his death on December 26, 1972, Truman was buried in the library courtyard. Bess Truman was laid next to him ten years later.

> "When you get to be President, there are all those things, the honors, the twenty-one gun salutes, all those things. You have to remember it isn't for you, it's for the Presidency."
> — Harry S. Truman

THE
PRESIDENTS
OF THE
UNITED STATES

George Washington
1789–1797

John Adams
1797–1801

Thomas Jefferson
1801–1809

James Madison
1809–1817

James Monroe
1817–1825

John Quincy Adams
1825–1829

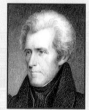
Andrew Jackson
1829–1837

Martin Van Buren
1837–1841

William Henry
Harrison
1841

John Tyler
1841–1845

James Polk
1845–1849

Zachary Taylor
1849–1850

Millard Filmore
1850–1853

Franklin Pierce
1853–1857

James Buchanan
1857–1861

Abraham Lincoln
1861–1865

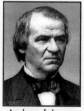
Andrew Johnson
1865–1869

Ulysses S. Grant
1869–1877

Rutherford B. Hayes
1877–1881

James Garfield
1881

Chester Arthur
1881–1885

Grover Cleveland
1885–1889

Benjamin Harrison
1889–1893

Grover Cleveland
1893-1897

William McKinley
1897–1901

Theodore Roosevelt
1901–1909

William H. Taft
1909–1913

Woodrow Wilson
1913–1921

Warren Harding
1921–1923

Calvin Coolidge
1923–1929

Herbert Hoover
1929–1933

Franklin D. Roo-
sevelt 1933–1945

Harry S. Truman
1945–1953

Dwight Eisenhower
1953–1961

John F. Kennedy
1961–1963

Lyndon Johnson
1963–1969

Richard Nixon
1969–1974

Gerald Ford
1974–1977

Jimmy Carter
1977–1981

Ronald Reagan
1981–1989

George H.W. Bush
1989–1993

William J. Clinton
1993–2001

George W. Bush
2001–

Note: Dates indicate years of
presidential service.
Source: www.whitehouse.gov

PRESIDENTIAL FACT FILE

THE CONSTITUTION

Article II of the Constitution of the United States outlines several requirements for the president of the United States, including:

* **Age:** The president must be at least 35 years old.

* **Citizenship:** The president must be a U.S. citizen.

* **Residency:** The president must have lived in the United States for at least 14 years.

* **Oath of Office:** On his inauguration, the president takes this oath: "I do solemnly swear (or affirm) that I will faithfully execute the office of President of the United States, and will to the best of my ability, preserve, protect and defend the Constitution of the United States."

* **Term:** A presidential term lasts four years.

PRESIDENTIAL POWERS

The president has many distinct powers as outlined in and interpreted from the Constitution. The president:

* Submits many proposals to Congress for regulatory, social, and economic reforms.

* Appoints federal judges with the Senate's approval.

* Prepares treaties with foreign nations to be approved by the Senate.

* Can veto laws passed by Congress.

* Acts as commander in chief of the military to oversee military strategy and actions.

* Appoints members of the cabinet and many other agencies and administrations with the Senate's approval.

* Can declare martial law (control of local governments within the country) in times of national crisis.

TRADITION

Many parts of the presidency developed out of tradition. The traditions listed below are but a few that are associated with the U.S. presidency.

★ After taking his oath of office, George Washington added, "So help me God." Numerous presidents since Washington have also added this phrase to their oath.

★ Originally, the Constitution limited the term of the presidency to four years, but did not limit the number of terms a president could serve. Presidents, following the precedent set by George Washington, traditionally served only two terms. After Franklin Roosevelt was elected to four terms, however, Congress amended the Constitution to restrict presidents to only two.

★ James Monroe was the first president to have his inauguration outside the Capitol. From his inauguration in 1817 to Jimmy Carter's inauguration in 1977, it was held on the Capitol's east portico. Ronald Reagan broke from this tradition in 1981 when he was inaugurated on the west portico to face his home state, California. Since 1981, all presidential inaugurations have been held on the west portico of the Capitol.

★ Not all presidential traditions are serious, however. One of the more fun activities connected with the presidency began when President William Howard Taft ceremoniously threw out the first pitch of the new baseball season in 1910.  Presidents since Taft have carried on this tradition, including Woodrow Wilson, who is pictured here as he throws the first pitch of the 1916 season. In more recent years, the president has also opened the All-Star and World Series games.

PRESIDENTIAL FACT FILE

THE WHITE HOUSE

Although George Washington was involved with the planning of the White House, he never lived there. It has been, however, the official residence of every president beginning with John Adams, the second U.S. president. The

building was completed approximately in 1800, although it has undergone several renovations since then. It was the first public building constructed in Washington, D.C. The White House has 132 rooms, several of which are open to the public. Private rooms include those for administration and the president's personal residence. For an online tour of the White House and other interesting facts, visit the official White House website, *http://www.whitehouse.gov.*

THE PRESIDENTIAL SEAL

A committee began planning the presidential seal in 1777. It was completed in 1782. The seal appears as an official stamp on medals, stationery, and documents, among other items. Originally, the eagle faced right toward the arrows (a symbol of war) that it held in its talons. In 1945, President Truman had the seal altered so that the eagle's head instead faced left toward the olive branch (a symbol of peace), because he believed the president should be prepared for war but always look toward peace.

President Truman in Profile

PERSONAL

Name: Harry S. Truman

Birth date: May 8, 1884

Birth place: Lamar, Missouri

Father: John Anderson Truman

Mother: Martha Ellen Young

Wife: Elizabeth "Bess" Virginia Wallace

Children: Mary Margaret Truman

Death date: December 26, 1972

Death place: Kansas City, Missouri

POLITICAL

Years in presidential office: 1945–1953

Vice president: Alben W. Barkley

Occupations before presidency: Farmer, judge, U.S. senator, vice president of the United States

Political party: Democrat

Major achievements of presidency: End of World War II, Truman Doctrine, Marshall Plan, Fair Deal and social reform efforts

Nickname: Give 'Em Hell Harry

Presidential library:

The Harry S. Truman Presidential Museum and Library
500 W. U.S. Highway 24
Independence, MO 64050
(800) 833-1225
http://www.trumanlibrary.org

Tributes:

The Harry S. Truman Memorial
   (Athens, Greece)

The Harry S. Truman National Historic Site
   (Independence and Grandview, Mo.; *http://www.nps.gov/hstr/*)

Harry S. Truman State Park
   (Warsaw, Mo.; *http://www.mostateparks.com/trumanpark.htm*)

1884 Harry S. Truman is born in Barton County, Missouri on May 8th.

1918 Truman is sent to France to fight in World War I and eventually gains command of Battery D; he marries Bess Wallace on June 28.

1922 Truman begins his political career when he is elected county court judge of eastern Jackson County.

1926 He is elected presiding judge of the county court.

1934 Truman is elected senator of Missouri.

1939 Germany invades Poland; World War II officially begins.

1941 Truman becomes chairman of the Committee to Investigate the National Defense Program; The United States enters World War II after Japan bombs Pearl Harbor.

1944 Franklin Roosevelt is elected to his fourth term as president, with Truman as vice president.

1945

April 13 Truman is sworn in as president after Roosevelt's death.

May 8 Germany surrenders.

July 17–August 2 Truman attends the Potsdam Conference.

August The atomic bombs "Little Boy" and "Fat Man" are dropped on Hiroshima and Nagasaki; Japan surrenders; World War II ends.

October 14 The UN Charter is ratified by involved countries.

1946 Steel, coal, and railroad workers strike, and all wage and price controls (except on rent, sugar, and rice) are ended.

1947 The Truman Doctrine is enacted, and $400 million in aid is given to Greece and Turkey; Congress overrides Truman's veto of the Taft–Hartley Act.

CHRONOLOGY

1948

April 3 Truman signs the Foreign Assistance Act of 1948, which begins implementation of Marshall Plan.

May 14 Truman recognizes the State of Israel.

June 26 The Berlin Airlift begins (the Russian blockade lasts until May 12, 1949, and the airlift officially ends on September 30, 1949).

July 26 Truman issues Executive Order 9981 to begin racial integration of the U.S. military and creates the President's Committee on Equality of Treatment and Opportunity in Armed Services (Fahy Committee).

November 2 Truman is narrowly elected to a second term.

1949

January Truman introduces "Fair Deal" proposals to Congress; "Point Four" is delivered in his State of Union Address; the North Atlantic Treaty Organization (NATO) is formed.

1950 North Korea invades South Korea; the United States enters the war on the side of South Korea; China enters on the side of North Korea. Two men attempt to assassinate Truman.

1951 Opposing forces reach a stalemate in Korea. The war ends on July 27, 1953.

1952 Truman signs treaties with Japan, Australia, New Zealand, and the Philippines; the United States tests the world's first thermonuclear bomb.

1957 The Harry S. Truman Museum and Library opens in Independence, Missouri.

1972 Truman dies at age 88 on December 26th and is buried in the Truman Library courtyard.

Bailey, Thomas A., and David M. Kennedy. *The American Spirit.* 6th edition, Vol 2. Lexington, Ky.: D.C. Heath and Company, 1987.

Donovan, Robert J. *Tumultuous Years: The Presidency of Harry S. Truman, 1949–1953.* New York: W.W. Norton, 1982.

Ferrel, Robert H. *Harry S. Truman and the Modern American Presidency.* Boston: Little, Brown, 1983.

Gardner, Michael R. *Harry Truman and Civil Rights: Moral Courage and Political Risks.* Carbondale, Ill.: Southern Illinois Press, 2002.

Goldman, Eric F. *The Crucial Decade: America, 1945–1955.* Westport, Conn.: Greenwood Press, 1956.

Jenkins, Roy. *Truman.* New York: Harper and Row Publishers, 1986.

Lowi, Theodore J., and Benjamin Ginsberg. *American Government: Freedom and Power.* Brief 5th edition. New York: W. W. Norton and Company, Inc. 1998.

McCoy, Donald R. *The Presidency of Harry S. Truman.* Lawrence, Kan.: University Press of Kansas, 1984.

Neal, Steve. *Harry and Ike: The Partnership that Remade the Postwar World.* New York: Scribner, 2002.

Poen, Monte M., ed. *Strictly Personal and Confidential: The Letters Harry Truman Never Mailed.* Columbia, Mo.: University of Missouri Press, 1999.

WEBSITES

Kevin Baker: The Temper Thing
http://www.kevinbaker.info/c_ttt.html

Truman Presidential Museum and Library
http://www.trumanlibrary.org/

USA Trivia: President Assassination Attempts
http://www.usatrivia.com/pasnatt.html

FURTHER READING

Collins, David R. *Harry S. Truman: People's President.* New York: Chelsea Juniors, 1991.

Faber, Doris. *Harry Truman.* New York: Abelard–Schuman, 1972.

Farley, Karin C. *Harry Truman: The Man from Independence.* Englewood Cliffs, N. J.: Julian Messner, 1989.

Hayman, Leroy. *Harry S. Truman: A Biography.* New York: Thomas Y. Crowell Company, 1969.

Hudson, Wilma J. *Harry S. Truman: Missouri Farm Boy.* New York: Bobbs–Merrill Co., 1973.

Leavell, J. Perry Jr. *Harry S. Truman.* New York: Chelsea House Publishers, 1988.

Steinberg, Alfred. *Harry S. Truman.* New York: G.P. Putnam's & Sons, 1963.

Acheson, Dean, 62, 63, 73, 76
Allied Powers, 24, 29–30
Anti-discrimination legislation, 66–70, 85
Antitrust legislation, 66
Armed services, desegregation of, 68–70
Asia, postwar policies, 54, 76, 81–82. *See also* Korean War
Assassination attempt, 86
Atomic bomb
  bombing of Japan, 29–31, 34, 36
  debate on use of, 31–35, 36–37
  first bomb detonated, 29
  Russia develops bomb, 72
Australia, 81
Axis Powers, 25

Battery D, 14
Belgium, 55
Benny, Jack, 87
Berlin airlift, 57
Berlin, Germany, 55–57
Blair House, 86
Britain, 50, 55, 56
Bush, George W., 8
Byrnes, James F., 49

Canada, 55
Capitalism, 23, 62–64
Carter, Jimmy, 86
Chiang Kai-Shek, 72
Chicago Tribune election headline, 60, 61
China
  becomes communist, 24, 53, 72
  division of Manchuria, 24
  enters Korean War, 78–79
Churchill, Winston, 25, 30
Civil rights legislation, 66–70, 85
Coal mining strikes, 43, 44
Cold war, 50, 54, 74, 80–84. *See also* Korean War

Collazo, Oscar, 86
Committee to Investigate the National Defense Program, 18
Communism
  containment in Asia, 54, 76, 81–82
  containment in Europe, 50–57
  economic system of Marx, 23–24
  fear of in U.S., 73–74
  spread of in Europe, 25, 30
  spread of to China, 24, 53, 72
Congress
  approval of Truman Doctrine, 52
  overrides veto of Taft–Hartley Act, 46
  postwar economic measures, 41–42
  Republican, elected in 1946, 42
  resists Fair Deal plan, 64–65, 84
  Truman calls special session in 1948, 59
Conservative viewpoint, 63–64
Constitution, presidential authority under, 8–9, 92
Containment policy, 50–57, 76, 81–82
County court judgeships, 15–16
Czech Republic, 55

Democratic Party, 58, 62–64
Democratic People's Republic of Korea, 74. *See also* North Korea
Denmark, 55
Desegregation of armed services, 68–70
Dewey, Thomas, 59–61
Dixiecrat Party, 58

Domestic policy
  economic policies, 38–42
  Fair Deal, 64–70, 84–85
  labor disputes, 40, 42–46, 65, 86–87
  New Deal, 21–23, 40
Domino theory, 51

Economy
  post–World War II, 38–42
  Roosevelt legacy, 21–23
  wartime boom, 38
Eisenhower, Dwight D., 58, 73, 80, 86
Elsey, George M., 70
Enola Gay, 29
Europe
  postwar policies on, 50–57
  postwar Russian influence in, 50–51, 55–57
  spread of communism in, 25, 30
Executive Order 9981 (EO 9981), 68–70

Fahy, Charles, 69
Fahy Committee, 69
Fair Deal
  civil rights legislation, 66–70, 85
  Congress blocks plan, 64–65, 84
  social reforms, 62–67, 84–85
"Fat Man," 31
Filibusters, 68
Foreign aid
  to Asia, 54, 81
  to Greece and Turkey, 50, 51–52
  to third world countries, 67, 70–71, 81
Foreign policy
  containment of communism, 50–57, 76, 81–82
  Marshall Plan, 48, 49, 53, 54

"Point Four" proposal, 67, 70–71
Roosevelt legacy, 23–26
Truman Doctrine, 48, 49, 54
Formosa (Taiwan), 72
France, 53, 55, 56

Germany, 24, 25, 29. *See also* West Germany
Grandview, Mo., 11, 12–13
Great Britain, 50, 55, 56
Great Depression, 20, 38, 40
Greece
  aid to, 50, 51–52
  communist threat to, 49, 50
  enters NATO, 55

H bomb. *See* Thermonuclear bomb
Harry S. Truman Museum and Library, 88, 89, 95
Hartley, Fred A., 46
Hiroshima, Japan, bombing of, 31, 34
Hume, Paul, 45
Hungary, 55
Hydrogen bomb. *See* Thermonuclear bomb

Iceland, 55
Independence, Mo., 11, 87, 89
India, 81
Inflation, postwar, 39–40, 41, 42
Isolationism, 83–84
Israel, recognition of, 58
Italy, 25, 53, 55

Japan
  atomic bombs dropped on, 29–31, 34
  cold war alliance with, 81
  50th anniversary of war, 36
  surrender of, 31, 33
  war in Pacific, 25, 28–29, 33

Jefferson, Thomas, 7–8
Judgeships, county court, 15–16

Kamikaze, 29
Kansas City, Mo., 12
Kim Il Sung, 74
Korea. *See* North Korea; South Korea
Korean War, 70, 74–80

Labor disputes, 40, 42–46, 65, 86–87
Labor unions, 43, 65
Laissez-faire economics, 23, 40, 42
Lamar, Mo., 10
Liberal viewpoint, 62–64
"Little Boy," 31
Louisiana Purchase, 7–8
Luxembourg, 55

MacArthur, Douglas, 77–80
Manchuria, 24
Mao Tse-Tung, 72
Marshall, George C., 49, 50, 53, 62
Marshall Plan, 48, 49, 53, 54
Marx, Karl, 23
Masons, 12
McCarthy, Joseph, 73
McCoy, Donald R., 65
Mfume, Kweisi, 70
Military buildup, during cold war, 81–84
Military services, desegregation of, 68–70
Minimum wage program, 66
Mining industry strikes, 40, 43
Mutual Security Act, 81

Nagasaki, Japan, bombing of, 31, 34
National Guard service, 13–14
National Labor Relations Act (1935), 46–47

National Security Council Memorandum Number 68 (NSC-68), 54, 82–84
NATO (North Atlantic Trade Organization), 54–55, 81
Netherlands, 55
New Deal, 21–23, 40
New Zealand, 81
North Atlantic Trade Organization (NATO), 54–55, 81
North Korea, 74, 75, 76
Norway, 55
NSC-68 (National Security Council Memorandum Number 68), 54, 82–84
Nuclear bomb. *See* Atomic bomb; Thermonuclear bomb

Okinawa, 33

Pacific war (World War II), 25, 28–29, 33
Pearl Harbor, 36
Pendergast, Jim, 15
Pendergast political machine, 15–17
People's Republic of China, 72. *See also* China
Plutonium bomb, 29, 31
"Point Four" proposal, 67, 70–71
Poland, 24, 25, 55
Policies. *See* Domestic policy; Foreign policy
Political parties, 58, 59, 62–64
Poll tax, 67
Portugal, 55
Potsdam Conference, 29–30
Potsdam Declaration, 29
Presidential authority, 8–9, 92
Presidential election (1948), 58–61

Presidential Fact File,
92–94
inauguration ceremony,
93
oath of office, 92, 93
presidential seal, 94
term of office, 92, 93
President's Committee on
Equality of Treatment
and Opportunity in the
Armed Services, 69
Presidents of the United
States, 90–91
Price controls, 41–42
Progressive Party, 58
Puerto Rico, 85, 86
Pyongyang, Korea, 78

Racism, 67, 68
Railroad strikes, 40, 43–45,
65
Railroads, seizure of,
44–45, 65
Rayburn, Sam, 39
"Red Scare," 73
Republic of Korea, 74.
See also South Korea
Republican Party, 59,
63–64
Rhee, Syngman, 74, 75
Roosevelt, Franklin D.
1944 election campaign,
18–19
death of, 20
political legacy of, 21–
27
at Yalta conference,
24–26
Russia. See also Cold war
atomic bomb as deterrent
to, 32
blockade of West Berlin,
55–57
develops atomic bomb,
72
develops hydrogen bomb,
84
influence in postwar
Europe, 50–51, 55–57

Potsdam Conference, 30
Warsaw Pact, 55
Yalta Conference, 24–26

Segregation, in armed
forces, 68–70
Seizures
railroads, 44–45, 65
steel mills, 7–8, 86
Senate
filibustering in, 68
Truman serves in, 16–18
Seoul, Korea, 77, 79
Social programs, 62–66, 67,
84–85
Social Security, 66, 67, 85
South Korea, 54, 74, 75
Soviet Union. See Russia
Spain, 55
Stalin, Joseph, 24, 25, 30
Steel industry strikes, 40,
43, 44, 86–87
Steel mills, seizure of, 7–8,
86
Stevenson, Adlai, 86
Strikes, 40, 42–46, 65,
86–87
Supreme Court decision on
steel mill seizure, 8, 86

Taft, Robert A., 46
Taft–Hartley Act, 46, 65, 86
Taiwan, 72
Thermonuclear bomb, 82,
84
Third world, aid to, 67,
70–71, 81
38th parallel, 79
Thurmond, Strom, 58, 60
Torresola, Griselio, 86
Truman Doctrine, 48, 49,
54
Truman, Elizabeth Wallace
("Bess")(wife), 13, 14, 89
Truman, Harry S.
assassination attempt on,
86
birth and early life,
10–13

business enterprises, 13,
15
death, 89
early political career,
15–16
facts and dates, 95–96
frustration with domestic
policy, 45–46, 64–66,
85
letters, 45
marriage, 13, 14
memoirs, 87
military service, 13–15
Presidential election
(1948), 58–61
retirement, 87–89
Senate terms, 16–18
sworn in as President
(1945), 22
vice presidency, 18–19,
26–27
Truman, John Anderson
(father), 10
Truman Library, 88, 89, 95
Truman, Martha Young
(mother), 10
Truman, Mary Margaret
(daughter), 13, 45
Turkey
aid to, 50, 51–52
communist threat to, 49,
50
enters NATO, 55

Unemployment, 39–40
Unions, labor, 43, 65
United Nations (UN), 35,
76
Uranium bomb, 31
U.S. Congress. See Congress
U.S. Senate. See Senate

Vice presidency, 18–19,
26–27
Vinson, Fred, 8

Wallace, Elizabeth Virginia.
See Truman, Elizabeth
Wallace

Wallace, Henry, 18, 58, 60
Warm Springs, Ga., 20
Warsaw Pact, 55
West Berlin, blockade of, 55–57
West Germany, 53, 55–56
White House, 94
World War I, 13–15
World War II
    atomic bombs dropped on Japan, 29–31, 34
    economic boom during, 38
    Germany surrenders, 29
    Japan surrenders, 31, 33
    Potsdam Conference, 29–30
    war contract investigation, 18
    war in Pacific, 25, 28–29, 33
    Yalta conference, 24–26

Yalta conference, 24–26
Yalu River, 77–78
Year of Decisions (Truman), 87
Years of Trial and Hope (Truman), 87
Young, Martha Ellen. *See* Truman, Martha Young
Youngstown v. Sawyer, 86

PICTURE CREDITS

ACKNOWLEDGMENTS

Thank you to Celebrity Speakers Intl. for coordinating Mr. Cronkite's contribution to this book.

Michael Foley is a freelance writer who lives and works in Philadelphia, Pennsylvania. His writings consist mainly of expository pieces relating to history and literature.

Walter Cronkite has covered virtually every major news event during his more than 60 years in journalism, during which he earned a reputation for being "the most trusted man in America." He began his career as a reporter for the United Press during World War II, taking part in the beachhead assaults of Normandy and covering the Nuremberg trials. He then joined *CBS News* in Washington, D.C., where he was the news anchor for political convention and election coverage from 1952 to 1980. CBS debuted its first half-hour weeknight news program with Mr. Cronkite's interview of President John F. Kennedy in 1963. Mr. Cronkite was inducted into the Academy of Television Arts and Sciences in 1985 and has written several books. He lives in New York City with his wife of 63 years.